Poetry Projects with Pizzazz!

15 Easy, Hands-on Poetry Activities That Invite Kids to Write and Publish Their Poems in Unique and Dazzling Ways

by Michelle O'Brien-Palmer

SCHOLASTIC
PROFESSIONAL BOOKS

New York • Toronto • London • Auckland • Sydney
Mexico City • New Delhi • Hong Kong • Buenos Aires

Dedication

This book is dedicated to the 130 young poets who
tested the poetry projects found inside these pages.
This book could not have been written without their
guidance. Thanks go to Corinne Richardson and her
third grade students at McAuliffe Elementary, Valerie
Marshall and Lee Ann Jackson and their fourth grade
students at Blackwell Elementary, Joyce Standing and
her fifth grade students at the Overlake School,
Sharie Hanson and her seventh grade students at
Redmond Junior High, and to John Pearson and his
seventh grade students at Evergreen Junior High.
I would also like to thank all the students who
submitted poetry samples and project samples.

Cover design by Norma Ortiz

Cover and interior photography by Donnelly Marks

Interior design by Sydney Wright

Interior illustrations by James Graham Hale

ISBN: 0-439-06496-1

Contents

Introduction

In classrooms across the country, teachers are reaching for poetry to help children play with language, exercise their imaginations, and explore their world. They use poetry to welcome the seasons and celebrate the curriculum. As poet Kathleen Hollenbeck explains: "When teachers reach for poetry, they know they will be heard."

Now you can help your young poets be heard as well. *Poetry Projects with Pizzazz* was written to help you inspire your students to express themselves through poetry. In the pages that follow, you'll find activities and opportunities to reach even your most reluctant writers. What makes this book so unique is that it was written with the help of over one hundred students in grades three through five. *Poetry Projects with Pizzazz* is a collection of our favorite projects, complete with project and poetry samples, simple poetry writing directions, and how-to steps to guide the way.

While there is no right or wrong way to introduce or implement these projects, we hope you and your students will find them inspirational. To begin, you may find it helpful to demonstrate how to write each new poetry form for your class, using the guidelines on page 54 as support. When your students are comfortable with the form, invite them to write individual, pair, or small group poems. Whether you use them as they are, or create your own innovations, we are sure that you and your students will be delighted with the projects and the poems. Have fun writing!

Poetry Journal

Students create personal poetry journals.

Eric Wright, a 5th-grade student, made this Poetry Journal.

Inspiration

The Poetry Journal is the perfect project for the beginning of any poetry unit. What better way to inspire students to write poetry than by inviting them to create a special book in which to do so?

Project Materials

- $9\frac{1}{2}$" by $9\frac{1}{2}$" pieces of decorative paper, such as wrapping paper
- 2 pieces of light cardboard per student, each $4\frac{1}{4}$" by $8\frac{1}{2}$"
- Scissors
- Rubber cement
- 30" pieces of $\frac{1}{8}$" wide ribbon
- $8\frac{1}{4}$" by $8\frac{1}{4}$" pieces of colored paper
- 4 pieces of lined writing paper cut to $7\frac{1}{2}$" wide by 8" long per student
- Extra-long stapler
- Pencils/pens/markers, art supplies
- Self-adhesive labels
- Rulers

Steps

1 Students should begin by placing wrapping paper face down on the table.

2 Next, have students place the two cardboard pieces on top of the wrapping paper, leaving a half-inch border around the outer edges and an eighth-inch space between the cardboard pieces.

3 Have students cut one small square out of each of the four corners of paper as shown. Then guide students in folding the corners of each piece of paper to form triangular flaps.

4 Next, have students attach the paper to the cardboard by folding the edges over and pasting them down with rubber cement.

5 Have students paste the ribbon to the center of the cover horizontally. Then have them glue the sheet of colored paper to the cardboard, covering the ribbon.

6 Once all the glue has dried, students should fold the writing paper in half lengthwise, being careful to align the lines for writing. Once the pages are folded and aligned, students should make a hard crease; then unfold the paper and staple the pages into the center of the cover to form the book's spine.

7 Have students write "My Poetry Journal" on their self-adhesive labels and invite them to decorate the label and cover in any way they wish.

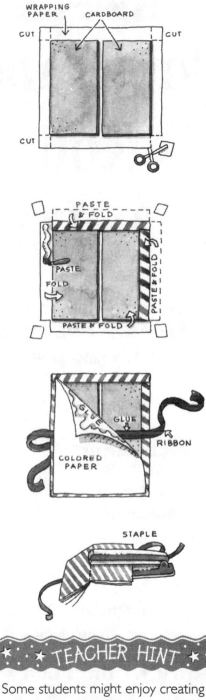

TEACHER HINT

Some students might enjoy creating their own writing or decorative paper for this project. Others might enjoy choosing decorative paper for their covers from a book of wallpaper samples. (You can get these free from many home-decorating stores or catalogs.)

Individual or Small Group

Wrap-and-Roll Poetry

Students write simple list poems as an introduction to non-rhyming poetry.

Sarah Breinig, Logan Aoki, Cameron Hodges, Alicia Reeves, and Ben Dulken—all 3rd-grade students—made this watermelon Wrap-and-Roll Poetry project together.

Project Materials

※ Pencils

※ Lined paper

※ Adding machine paper (one 12" to 15" long piece per student or group)

※ Lidded cans with safe edges and a plastic lid ("International Coffee" cans work well)

※ Tape

※ Art supplies (ribbon, glitter, feathers, markers, and stickers)

※ Exacto™ knife (adult supervision required)

Poetry Writing: List Poems

1 Invite children to select a subject for their poem. Then have them write the first word that comes to mind about their subject on a sheet of lined paper. Explain that this word will be the first word of their poem.

2 Encourage children to continue writing their poem by composing a list of ten words that describe their topic.

3 Have children think of titles for their poems and then set them aside.

My Dog Maya
Cute
Jealous
Kind
Furry
Loving
Silly
Mischievous
Fast
Frisky
Friendly
—Dane Steel, Grade 4

Project Steps

1 Have children write the title of their poems and their names about two inches from the top of the piece of adding-machine paper.

2 In the remaining space, have children rewrite their poems, adding any illustrations they would like.

3 Help children create covers for their cans by taping two layers of adding machine paper to the outside of each one. Once children have attached the paper, they can decorate their cans.

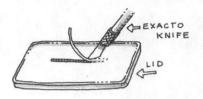

4 Using an Exacto™ knife, cut a rectangle in the center of each plastic lid. The rectangle must be wide enough to allow the adding machine paper to roll out of the lid easily. (Because this step involves using a sharp instrument, it should be completed by an adult.)

5 Next, students should roll up their poems and place them in the cans. Show students how to thread the top of the poem through the rectangular slot in the lid before placing the lid back on the can.

6 Invite students to share their poems with friends and families.

★ ○ ○ ○ ○ **project Extension** ○ ○ ○ ○ ★

Invite students to make poetry cans about people, places, or events you are studying as part of a social studies unit. This project is also ideal for highlighting animals and environments you are studying in science.

Getting- to-Know- You Mobiles

Students create poetry mobiles using simple name or acrostic poems to introduce people, places, and events they have come to know.

The Oregon Trail served as the theme of this Getting-to-Know-You Pioneer Mobile designed by 4th-grade students.

Project Materials

❋ Pencils/pens

❋ Draft paper

❋ Final acrostic poems

❋ Skein of yarn

- Two 4" pieces of yarn per group
- Two 36" pieces of yarn per group

❋ 1 hanger per group

❋ Scissors

❋ 2 pieces of construction paper or card stock (1 per student)

❋ Hole punch

❋ Photographs or illustrations of each partner

❋ Glue

Poetry Writing: Name or Acrostic Poems

1 Each Getting-to-Know-You mobile shares information for about four students. To get started, divide the class into groups of four. Then, have each student pick a partner to begin the poetry writing process.

2 Have each child list the letters of his partner's name in a column going down the left-hand side of a sheet of lined paper.

3 Then invite students to interview their partners to get some ideas of what to include in their poems.

4 Once students feel they have gathered enough information about their partners, have them compose their poems by writing a word or sentence that begins with each letter in the column.

5 When students are happy with their poems, have them type them on the computer or write them out carefully on another sheet of lined paper.

5th-grader Meredith Yaxley wrote this acrostic poem about her classmate Hope Strater:

Hyper Hope
Outgoing
Pal to everyone
Excited

Super
Terrific
Radical
Awesome
Tremendously extreme
Excellent
Radical

Project Steps

1 Have one student in each group wind the the skein of yarn around the hanger. Once the hanger is completely covered, have students tie the end into a small knot and cut away any remaining yarn.

YARN

2 Next, students should punch a hole in the top center of their card-stock piece.

3 Invite students to cut the acrostic poem into an interesting shape before they paste it onto the front of the card stock piece. Students should then paste a photograph or an illustration of their partner to the opposite side of the card-stock piece.

4 Have students thread a piece of yarn around the base of the hanger and then thread it through the hole in their card-stock piece, securing it with a knot. Be sure each member of the group uses different lengths of yarn when attaching card-stock pieces so that the pieces do not bump into one another.

5 Hang mobiles on a clothesline or from the ceiling. Then, invite each group of students to share their mobile with the class, giving everyone an opportunity to get to know one another.

★ ○ ○ ○ ○ Project Extension ○ ○ ○ ○ ★

Use this project to help students get to know each other at the beginning of the year. Getting-to-Know-You Mobiles are also a fun way to enhance science, foreign language, and language arts units.

Whole Class or Small Groups

Poetry Puzzles

Introduce students to the art of alliteration with these poetry jigsaw puzzles.

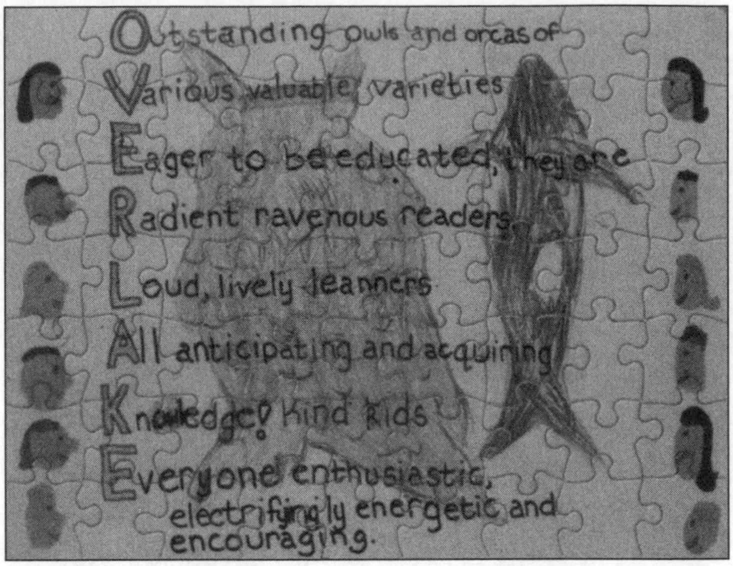

Outstanding owls and orcas of
Various valuable varieties
Eager to be educated, they are
Radient ravenous readers,
Loud, lively leanners
All anticipating and acquiring
Knowledge! Kind kids
Everyone enthusiastic,
electrifyingly energetic and
encouraging.

The 5th-grade students at the Overlake School designed this Poetry Puzzle.

Project Materials

- Pencils/pens/markers
- Draft paper
- 10 1/2" by 13 1/4" Compose-a-Puzzle (available at most teacher-supply stores). You can also provide students with pieces of cardboard or card stock in the same dimensions.
- Art supplies (paints, glitter, etc.)
- 1 small plastic container or envelope to store each puzzle

Poetry Writing: Acrostic Alliteration

1. Before students begin working on their poems, you may need to introduce or review the term *alliteration*—a series of words starting with the same sound such as "one wild wacky wonderful weekend." Explain to students that, like list poems, these poems need not rhyme.

2. Invite your class to work together to create an acrostic alliteration poem about someone or something important to them all. (See the sample on the next page.) You may want to provide students with dictionaries to assist them in their writing.

Corrine Richardson's 3rd-grade students wrote this poem about themselves as writers:

> Wonderful, wacky writers
> Rhyming, reading, and rad
> Interesting, intelligent, and full of ideas
> They're terrific, talented talkers
> Eager, excellent, energetic editors
> Respectful, responsible revisers and
> Special, super-sensational students!

★☆TEACHER HINT☆★

Use the poetry puzzle as a morale booster to promote classroom/school unity and pride. If you cannot find these puzzles in your local craft store or teacher-supply store, visit HYPERLINK www.compozapuzzle.com on the Internet.

Project Steps

1 Once the class has drafted a poem, select a student to copy the poem onto the puzzle board or card stock.

2 Next, have students pick three or four classmates to decorate the poetry puzzle in a way that reflects its subject.

3 After the artwork has dried, have students either break their puzzle pieces apart or cut their cardboard or card stock into puzzle pieces. Then have students place their puzzles into the container or envelope.

4 Invite students to break into smaller poetry puzzle-making groups. Once they have made group puzzles following the steps above, have groups exchange and assemble each other's puzzles.

★ ∘ ∘ ∘₀ **Project Extension** ₀∘ ∘ ∘ ★

Try writing a group poem about a science or social studies topic that you've just studied.

Alicia Reeves, a 3rd-grade student
made this Poetry Spinner.

Project Materials

※ Pencils/pens/markers

※ Draft paper

※ Glue

※ Page 50 copied onto 4 different complementary colors of card stock

※ Art supplies (stickers, glitter etc.)

※ Laminating machine (If you do not have access to a laminating machine, you can
have children paste their spinners to a piece of card stock or a manila folder for
added durability.)

※ Scissors

※ Stick pins

※ ⅛" thick balsa wood sticks (about 8" long)

※ Earring clutch or small circular eraser

Poetry Writing: Free-form Poetry

1 Before students begin to write their poems, clear a space in your classroom or take
children outside (or somewhere else) where they can spread out, close their eyes,
stretch out their arms and spin freely. As they do, ask them to pay close attention to
the feeling of their movements and of the air as it rushes all around them.

2 Once children are back in the classroom, ask them to recall and reflect on the words that came to mind as they twirled and spun. Invite them to use these words to compose three or four lines of free-form poetry that become progressively shorter.

Spin. You go faster no longer on earth, but dancing in the clouds.
Fly with birds, walk on a rainbow,
Slowly stopping, flying, but dancing in the clouds.

—Erin Kelly, Grade 5

Project Steps

1 Have students cut out the four card-stock circles and then glue them together—placing the smallest circle in the center of the next largest circle and so on—until all four circles are on top of one another, forming four rings.

2 Ask students to copy the first line of their poem inside the largest ring, the second line in the next ring and so on, until students are left with one small circle in the middle of the spinner.

3 Invite students to decorate their spinners with stickers, artwork, and glitter to make them festive.

4 If you have access to a laminator, laminate students' spinners.

5 Help students attach their spinners to the balsa wood by poking the stick pin through the very center of the spinner into the top 1/2" of the balsa wood piece.

6 Place the earring clutch or eraser over the point of the stick pin to keep it from hurting anyone.

★ **TEACHER HINT** ★

Display students' spinners on a bulletin board to make a beautiful, hands-on, classroom poetry display. Just omit the earring clutch or eraser and push the stick pins directly into the bulletin board.

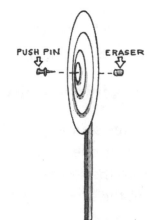

PUSH PIN   ERASER

Individual or Partners

Poetry Corners

Students create their own ideal writing space and experiment with short rhyming poetry at the same time.

This Poetry Corner was designed by 4th-graders Olivia Zimmerman and Rebecca Harlin.

Project Materials

- Draft paper
- Pencils/pens
- Shoe box (or a similar square box) for each student
- Art supplies to decorate and furnish each box (decorative paper, carpet samples, stickers, cardboard, clay)
- Rubber cement or glue
- Scissors
- Small pieces of white paper
- Small pieces of construction paper for a frame

Poetry Writing: Quatrains

Quatrains are stanzas or entire poems composed of four rhyming lines. Typically, the rhymes follow one of two patterns: with *abba*, the first and fourth lines rhyme with each other, as do the second and third lines. With *abab*, the first and third lines form a rhyming pair, as do the second and fourth lines. Some quatrains are written according to yet another pattern: *aabb*. In this pattern, the first two lines rhyme with each other as do the last two.

(*abba structure*)
This is my writing place,
Just like my writing room.
Where all my words bloom.
Where I keep my own pace.
—Jordan Loftli, Grade 3

(*aabb structure*)
Writing poetry high in the sky,
Above the mountains and oceans I lie.
Inspired by sunsets and the world below,
I write poems for the loved ones I know.
—Christina Caporale, Grade 5

1 Once you've introduced students to the patterns of rhyming quatrains, invite them to imagine the ideal writing place. Ask: What does it look like? What does it feel like to be in this place? What about it makes you want to write there?

2 Have students write a quatrain poem on draft paper describing this imaginary place using one of the rhyming structures described above.

★ TEACHER HINT ★

This corner makes a fun homework project. Parents really enjoy helping their children find meaningful material samples, wrapping paper scraps, and other needed items. This project is also great in that it gives you some real insights into what inspires your young writers.

Project Steps

1 Ask students to begin by drawing a detailed plan for their corners on a piece of paper. Each plan should include furniture, artwork, and whatever else students feel they would like to have in their spaces. As students work on their plans, be sure to remind them to allot space for a small framed version of their quatrain.

2 Once students' plans are complete, invite them to gather the materials they feel are necessary to construct and decorate their corners inside their shoeboxes.

3 When students' corners are nearly complete, have them copy their quatrain poems onto small pieces of paper. Then have them make small frames using construction paper to fit around their poems.

4 Once students have hung or glued their poems into their corners, have them share their projects and poetry with the class. Ask: What about this place makes it fun for you to write poetry? What materials did you use to decorate your project? Why?

✦ ○ ○ ○ Project Extension ○ ○ ○ ○ ✦

The students in John Pearson's class at Evergreen Junior High designed Poetry Corners that reflected significant events in American history. Their quatrain poetry featured important information about each event.

Individual or Partners

Inkblot Poetry

Students write couplet poems inspired by their own inkblot artwork.

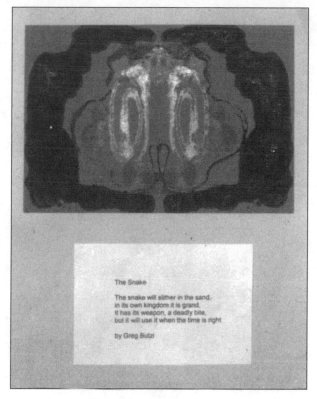

The Snake

The snake will slither in the sand,
in its own kingdom it is grand,
it has its weapon, a deadly bite,
but it will use it when the time is right.

by Greg Butzi

Greg Butzi, a 5th-grade student, created this Inkblot poetry project about a snake.

The snake will slither in the sand,
in its own kingdom it is grand.
It has its weapon, a deadly bite,
but it will use it when the time is right.

Project Materials

�֎ Smocks or aprons (optional)

✖ Draft paper

✖ Pencils/pens

✖ 5" by 4" colored construction paper

✖ 8½" by 11" colored construction paper (complementary to the smaller paper)

✖ 3 to 5 bottles of shiny fabric paint (tempera paint can be substituted if necessary)

✖ Glue

✖ Scissors

✖ Glitter

✖ White paper (4" by 10")

Poetry Writing: Couplets

Couplets almost always rhyme. They are usually formed by writing two lines of rhyming poetry.

Horsefly

I see a big horsefly
Sitting in an apple pie.
When it takes a big bite
It will slip right out of sight.
—*Laurel Shull, Grade 3*

Under the Sun

Under the sun we like to write,
Just you and me all day and night.
—*Elliot Lee and Blake Siezworth, Grade 4.*

In this activity, students will use their inkblot artwork as the inspiration for writing two lines of rhyming poetry—that is to say, a couplet.

Project and Poetry Writing Steps

1 Explain that students will use the artwork they create as inspiration for a couplet poem. Note: Younger students may need to put on smocks or aprons before beginning.

2 Once students have chosen their paper and paint, ask them to fold the small piece of colored construction paper in half along the 5-inch side.

PAINT DROPS

3 Have students unfold the construction paper and place five large drops of paint into the middle of the paper. Then ask them to fold the paper together again, rubbing the side of the paper gently so that the paint does not spill out.

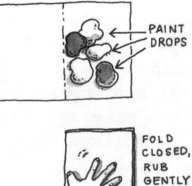

FOLD CLOSED, RUB GENTLY

TEACHER HINT

Invite students to experiment with different textured paints in making their inkblots. One class added glitter to the paint to create an interesting texture and a whole new poetry inspiration.

4 Next, invite students to open up the painted paper and place it on a flat surface to dry. While it dries, students may begin the poetry-writing process.

5 Once students have written drafts of their poems, have them rewrite these in final form on white paper. Be sure that students include their names and poem titles.

6 After students' artwork has dried, ask them to glue their inkblot designs to the tops of the large sheets of construction paper. Then have them glue their poems into the space below.

★○°○°project Extension ○°○°○★

This artwork can be used to inspire many different types of writing. Students can write stories using three to six inkblot paintings as the foundation for their entire story. Save students' inkblot paintings in a basket and invite the class to select a piece at random to use as a writing prompt or story starter.

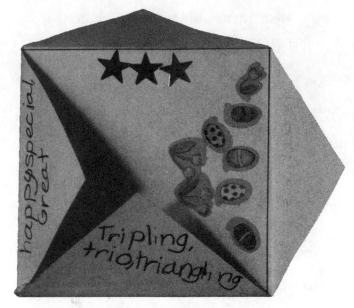

Sarah Breinig, Cameron Hodges, Stephanie MacDonald, Danielle Morris, and Jordan Softli all 3rd-grade students—worked together to create this Best-Guess Poetry Square.

Individual or Partners

Best-Guess Poetry Square

Students increase their vocabularies and strengthen their math skills with cinquain poetry.

Poetry and Project Materials

- ✄ Draft paper
- ✄ Pencils/pens/markers
- ✄ One copy of page 51 per student
- ✄ Scissors
- ✄ Art supplies (paint, stickers, fabric pieces, carpet samples, etc.)

Poetry Writing: Cinquain Poems

A cinquain poem is composed of five short, non-rhyming lines:

Line 1—One-word title

Line 2—Two descriptive words

Line 3—Three action words

Line 4—Four feeling words (how I feel when I think about the title)

Line 5—Another word that describes the title

In this particular project, the last line will be the number or concept the poem describes—
the answer to the riddle.

> Triple
> Few, Tres
> Tripling, Trio, Triangling
> Happy, Special, Great, Friends
> Answer: #3
> > —Sarah Breining, Danielle Morris, Jordan Softli, Stephanie MacDonald,
> > and Cameron Hodges, Grade 3

> Bronze
> Tricycle, Triangle
> Winning, Wheeling, Angling
> Happy, Friendly, Fun-loving, Learning
> Answer: #3
> > —Dane Steel and Nic Bruya, Grade 4

1 Have the class vote to select the number or math concept they will use as the subject of their guessing poem. This number or concept will become the last line of their poem, the one the readers must guess.

2 Next, invite students to think of clues (descriptive words, action words, etc.) to use in their poems. Record these words on the board.

3 Have your class write a group poem about the number or math concept they chose following the structure outlined above.

4 Break the class into groups of four or five. Then invite each group to select a new number and work together to write a draft of a group poem—leaving the last line off so readers can guess the answer number of the poem.

Project Steps

1 Distribute a copy of page 51 to each group and have students cut out the poetry square.

2 Next, show students how to fold each of the square's corners into its center, making a hard crease on each dotted line.

3 Using the project sample from the book and page 51 as your guide, help students write each of the first four lines of the poem on one of the folded triangles, working clockwise so that the first line goes in the upper left-hand corner, the second in the upper right-hand corner, the third in the lower right-hand corner, and the fourth in the lower left-hand corner. Write the fifth line on the back of the poetry square.

4 Have students lift each triangle and draw pictures or paste stickers on the inside of each one to represent the words on the outside flap.

5 When everyone has finished their cinquain squares, have students exchange them to see if they can guess what each other's poems are about.

★ ○ ○ ○ ○ Project Extension ○ ○ ○ ○ ★

The Best-Guess Poetry Square is a great tool for reinforcing students' understanding of science concepts, historical events, language arts, and even foreign languages.

Triorama Poetry

Students celebrate favorite topics with haiku poetry inside trioramas.

Kate Lovell, a 4th-grader, based her historical haiku and triorama on the Oregon Trail.

Project Materials

※ Draft paper

※ Pencils/pens

※ 4 copies of page 52 per student

※ Art supplies (paint, stickers, fabric pieces, carpet samples, clay, etc.)

※ 3 to 5 bottles of shiny fabric paint (tempera paint can be substituted if necessary)

※ Glue

※ Yarn or fishing wire

Poetry Writing: Haiku

Haiku is a major form of Japanese poetry that is composed of three lines and seventeen syllables. The first and third lines of a haiku have five syllables. The second line has seven.

1 Begin this project by inviting your class to select a topic for their haikus and trioramas. Let your class know that you will first work together to write a class haiku. Then, each member of the class will create a triorama to display his or her own haiku poetry.

2 Review with your students how to break words into syllables. Then, discuss the fact that, in a haiku, the first and third lines have five syllables while the second line has seven.

3 Using the above guidelines, write a class haiku. Your students can use this writing activity as a model for the project steps that follow. This haiku was written by Corrine Richardson's 3rd-graders and is based on the book *Mufaro's Beautiful Daughters*:

>Two in a garden
>A forest full of magic
>Nyoka's palace

This haiku by 5th-grader Hannah Rivenburgh was based on the book *Harry Potter and the Sorcerer's Stone*:

>Cupboard beneath stairs
>Happy but busy; Hogwarts
>Dungeons, spells, and tricks

Project Steps

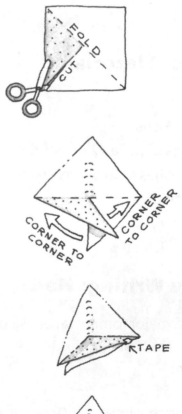

1 Have students cut out the squares from their copies of page 52. Ask them to cut and fold the squares into four-triorama panels

2 Invite students to write the title and each line of their haiku on separate pieces of white paper.

3 Once students have finished writing out their haiku, they should draw scenery in the top larger panel of each triorama to act as backdrops for each line of poetry.

4 When the scenery is in place, invite students to create three-dimensional scenes on the bottom panel of each triorama to bring each line of their haiku to life.

5 Once students have finished decorating their trioramas, have them attach all four along the back spines with glue.

6 Next, students should attach the title and each line of poetry to its corresponding triorama scene.

7 Have your students punch a hole at the top of the triorama. Then, ask students to thread fishing line or yarn through the hole. Finally, hang each student's triorama from the ceiling and invite each student to share his or her haiku.

★ ★ TEACHER HINT ★ ★

Be sure students finish decorating all four trioramas before they glue them all together. It is much more difficult to decorate them once they are a unit.

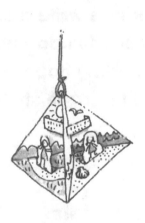

AFTER DECORATING, GLUE BACK-TO-BACK

★ ∘ ∘ ∘ ∘ project Extension ∘ ∘ ∘ ∘ ★

Students can create scientific haiku as well, making trioramas that highlight the habitats of different animals. Students might also enjoy creating haiku and trioramas that feature scenes from a favorite book.

Pleated Pop-Up Poetry

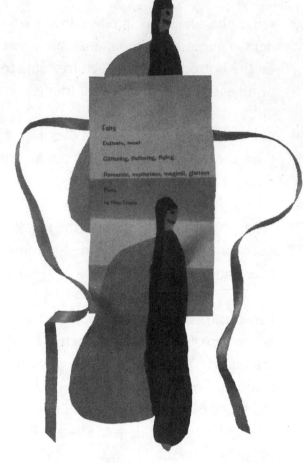

Students write cinquain poems in a fun pop-up format inspired by Hope Strater, a 5th-grade student.

This Pleated Pop-Up Poem about a fairy was made by 5th-grader Hope Strater.

Project Materials

- ❋ Draft paper
- ❋ Pencils/pens
- ❋ Construction paper for pop-up design
- ❋ Rubber cement or glue
- ❋ 1 piece of 6" by 2" white paper per student
- ❋ Extra-wide craft sticks (approximately 6" by ³/₄" wide)
- ❋ one 12" piece of ¹/₄" thick ribbon per student

Poetry Writing

A cinquain poem is composed of five short, non-rhyming lines.
Line 1—One-word title
Line 2—Two descriptive words (adjectives)

Line 3—Three action words (verbs)

Line 4—Four feeling words (how I feel when I think about the title)

Line 5—Another word that describes the title

1 Using the format above, invite each student to write a cinquain poem about a story character, person, animal, or thing that is important to them.

2 As students work, encourage them to think of ways they can illustrate their poems in pop-up form.

Pizza
Hot, yummy
Warm, melting, eating
Happy, hungry, refreshing, filling
Cheesy

—*Doug Babcock, Grade 4*

Dogs
Cute, cuddly
Cuddling, playing, barking
Happy, special, playful, great
Animal

—*Lindsey Rose, Grade 3*

Project Steps

1 Have students create front and back covers for their pop-up poems using construction paper or card stock. The pop-up cover should be between 5" and 7" tall and between 3" and 4" wide. Each student should design one cover, cut it out, and then trace it to create the second cover. Invite students to decorate their pop-up covers.

FRONT COVER

BACK COVER

2 Show students how to use an accordion fold to divide the 6" long strip of white paper into 1" long folded sections.

3 Have students write their names inside the first fold and the titles of their poems inside the second fold. Next, students should write one line of poetry inside each of the remaining folds, leaving the last fold empty.

4 Ask students to glue the back cover of the pop-up to the back of the craft stick. Help them to center the cover so that the top half is above the stick and the bottom half is glued to the stick.

5 Next, students should attach their cinquain strips to their craft sticks by gluing the first fold over the stick and the cover so that their names and poem titles show.

6 Have each student fold the ribbon in half to find its center. Then ask them to glue a center section of the ribbon to the back of the front cover of the pop-up. Each student should then glue the ribbon in the center of the cover.

7 Help students to align the two covers and then ask them to paste the last section of the poem over the ribbon on the back of the pop-up cover, leaving it face up to dry. Once students have read their poems, they can close their pop-ups by tying the ribbon around the back cover, behind the craft stick.

Rick F. } 1"
Butterfly

BACK COVER

GLUE

GLUE

Rick F.
Butterfly

GLUE LAST POEM PANEL TO BACK OF FRONT COVER

Rick F.
Butterfly

Poetic Number Line

Corrine Richardson's 3rd-grade class made this Poetic Number Line together. They chose leaf shapes to complement their study of forests.

Students work in groups to create poetic number lines or poetry using numbers and alliteration.

Project Materials

- ✸ Draft paper
- ✸ Pencils/pens
- ✸ 5 Sheets of 6" by 2½" white paper
- ✸ 5 pieces of 9" by 5½" colored construction paper
- ✸ Glue
- ✸ Tape
- ✸ 2 yards of thick, colored yarn

Poetry Writing

1 Divide your class into groups of four or five students. Ask each group to choose a general subject area for their line poem project.

2 One member of each group needs to write the numbers 1 through 5 in a column down the left-hand side of a sheet of draft paper.

3 Once students have written each number, ask them to think about the initial sound of each, starting with the number 1. As a class, compose a list of words that begin with the same /w/ sound, such as *wonderful, worry, wise, weird,* etc.

4 Challenge students to write a sentence using these and other words with the /w/ sound.

5 Have groups go through the same process for each number.

> One wiggly, wobbly wombat wondered why
> Two tacky tortoises traveled to Thailand together.
>
> Three thundering thrashing sharks ate
> Four flying flounder fish for a feast.
>
> Five ferocious foxes found
> Six slithering snakes sleeping in the sun.
>
> Seven spying spiders spied on
> Eight angry agitated alligators.
> —*Anna Gordon, Majd Shabaneh, Dane Steel,*
> *Richard Yagi, and Olivia Zimmerman, Grade 4*

The Lewis and Clark Expedition
One exciting, enthusiastic expedition was led by
Two tremendous, tireless friends who traveled

Three thronging, thrashing, rivers as at least
Four fabulous falls were forded.

Five friendly tribes were led by Jefferson, the Great White father.
Six serious men sought a sly, smart prairie dog.

Seven more sluggish steps in sand to the sea and
Eight exhausted men arrived home.
> —*Hannah Rivenburgh and Andrew Cocanour, Grade 5*

Project Steps

1 Have students reread their poems and create a shape to highlight each line of poetry. For example, Corrine Richardson's class decided to use a leaf shape to highlight each line of their poem.

2 Once students have created a shape for each line, they should transfer it to colored construction paper and cut it out, leaving a 1-inch tab at the top.

3 Invite students to write each line of their poem on a piece of white paper. Students can either cut their poems apart and paste the lines to the corresponding shapes they have created, or they can trace the shapes onto the white paper, cut them out, and then write the lines of their poem within the shapes.

4 Once students have written out their poems and glued them to the corresponding construction paper shapes, have them fold the tabs over and tape them to the back of the shapes creating paper loops.

5 Next, guide students in weaving the yarn through the tabs at the top of each shape in numerical order. Then hang Poetic Number Lines on a clothesline or around the edges of your room for all to see.

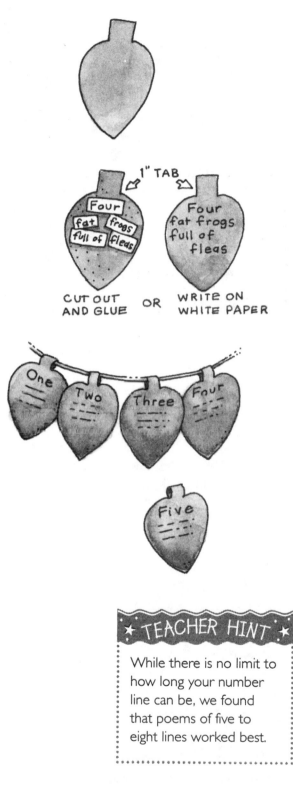

TEACHER HINT

While there is no limit to how long your number line can be, we found that poems of five to eight lines worked best.

Straw-Painting Poetry

Students write haiku poems using their straw art as an inspiration.

In the big blue sky
Wild shiny fireworks fly high
Telling I'm special

—Kim Harrison, Grade 4

Project Materials

- Draft paper
- Pencils/pens
- Aprons
- 2 different colors of watered-down tempera paint (1 part paint to 3 parts water)
- Spoons
- Straws
- White card stock or plain sheets of 8½" by 11" white paper
- Small sheets of white paper (4" by 3")
- Scissors
- Glue

Poetry Writing

This project is fun but can get rather messy. Be sure to give children smocks and cover your work surface with newspaper or a plastic tablecloth before starting. You may also want to

experiment with different kinds of paper as different weights and textures can add interesting effects.

Haiku

Haiku is a major form of Japanese poetry that is composed of three lines and seventeen syllables. The first and third lines of a haiku have five syllables; the second line has seven.

Raining Paint

What a mess this is.
Paint is flying everywhere.
Nature's raining paint.

—Brandon Rhoads, Grade 3

Wind

Branches attacking
No room to hide because it's
Very dangerous

—Stephen Waite, Grade 5

For this project, students will use the artwork they create following the steps below to inspire their haiku poems.

Project Steps

1 Make sure that surfaces and students' clothing are properly protected.

2 Have each student drop a small spoonful of paint onto the card stock or paper.

3 Invite students to blow through their straw gently to move the paint around the page. Have them blow through the straw at different angles to make their designs as distinctive as possible.

4 As students allow their artwork to dry, ask them to think about the designs they have created and what they look like to them. Give each student a piece of draft paper and have them compose a haiku inspired by their straw painting. Remind students that the first and third lines of their poem should have five syllables, with seven syllables in the second line.

5 Once students have composed haikus they are happy with, invite them to copy their poems onto the small sheets of white paper.

6 Have students paste their poetry onto their straw paintings. Some students may wish to cut their poems into shapes before pasting them down to accentuate their designs. If you'd like, you can have students mount their paintings and poems onto a larger piece of colored construction paper.

> ★ TEACHER HINT ★
>
> While the Straw-Painting Poetry project is usually done individually, it also makes a great group project if you use large sheets of butcher paper instead of the smaller pieces of white paper.

Small Groups

Magnetic Poetry

Students work in small groups to compose non-rhyming poems about an issue or area of the curriculum they have studied together.

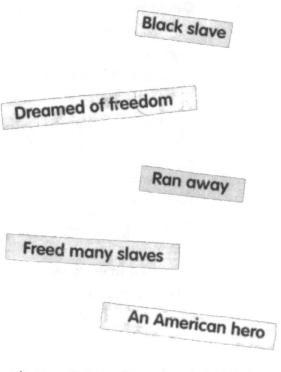

Black slave

Dreamed of freedom

Ran away

Freed many slaves

An American hero

This Magnetic Poetry project was made by the 5th-grade students in Joyce Standing's classroom.

Project Materials

- ✹ Draft paper
- ✹ Pencils/pens
- ✹ Computer and printer
- ✹ Coil of self-adhesive magnet
- ✹ Scissors
- ✹ Magnetic board

Poetry Writing

Tanka (tanhg-kuh) is a classic form of Japanese poetry that dates back at least 1,300 years. Tanka poems are composed of five unrhymed lines. Today's tanka takes on many forms. The tanka poetry presented in this activity counts words instead of syllables. It follows a 2-, 3-, 2-, 3-, 3- words per line format. Like the traditional tanka, the lines of the poem when read together form a single complete thought.

Geology

Rocks, minerals
Igneous, metamorphic, sedimentary
Sandstone, limestone
Marble, granite, slate
Diamond, pyrite, galena
—*Corrine Richardson's 3rd-graders*

Wetlands

Fragile habitat
Muddy, soggy, grassy
Nature's home
Important to everyone
Handle with care
—*Valerie Marshall's 4th-graders*

1 Select a subject for the whole class to write about and then divide the class into groups of four or five. Have each group select one member to be its recorder.

2 Ask students to brainstorm a list of statements to describe the topic. Then have them use those statements to compose their tanka.

Project Steps

1 If you have access to a computer, have each group type their poem, leaving at least six spaces between each line. (If you do not have access to a computer, simply have one member of each group copy the lines of poetry onto white paper.)

2 Once students have typed or written out their poems, have them cut the lines into 1-inch widths to fit the magnet.

3 Assist students in cutting the magnetic strips to the length of each line of poetry.

4 Have students peel the self-adhesive tape off of the cut magnets and carefully place the poetry lines onto the magnetic strips.

MAGNET

5 Place students' poems on a magnetic board where the class can enjoy them.

6 Once students have had an opportunity to admire each poem in its original form, invite them to create new tankas using strips from their classmates' poems as well as their own. Be sure to record all of the poems students create on a piece of chart paper or in a class poetry collection.

Individual

Poem-Teller

Students record and share information about a person, place, or thing in a fun and familiar guessing-game format.

This Poem-Teller was made by 3rd-grader Danielle Morris.

Project Materials

- Draft paper
- Pencils/pens
- One copy of page 53 per student

Famous
Black
Loved
Serious
Aperson who changed the World.
Answer: Martin Luther King, Jr.

Poetry Writing

These "guess the person, place, or thing" poems offer descriptive one-word clues in lines one to four, a descriptive sentence in line five, and the answer in line six.

Hot
Beaches
Swimmers
Scuba diving
In the State of Florida
Miami

—Valerie Marshall's 4th-graders

Leader
Expedition
Explorer
Journalist
Secretary to Thomas Jefferson
Meriwether Lewis
—*Rita Kanagat, Grade 5*

1 To create a Poem-Teller, each student will need to write two poems using the following format:

descriptive word
descriptive word
descriptive word
statement
answer

2 Once students have selected a subject for each of their poems, have them write drafts.

Project Steps

1 Have students fold the square sheet of paper in half four directions as shown.

2 Next, students should fold the corners in toward the center, so that the Poem-Teller looks like the diagram at right.

3 Have students open up the folded paper and write both of their poems in the triangular shapes as designated.

4 Once students have written their poems in the spaces, have them refold their Poem-Teller and then share it with a friend.

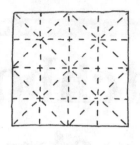

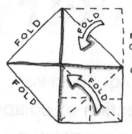

FOLD EACH CORNER TO CENTER OF SQUARE.

FLIP OVER THEN FOLD EACH CORNER TO CENTER OF SQUARE AGAIN.

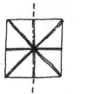

FOLD IN HALF HORIZONTALLY, THEN UNFOLD.

FOLD IN HALF VERTICALLY, THEN UNFOLD.

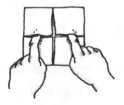

FLIP OVER INSERT INDEX FINGERS AND THUMBS UNDER THE FLAPS. TURN UPRIGHT.

POP UP!

Matchbook Poetry

Students create a collection of compact, free-form poetry pieces to highlight a person or a place related to a larger theme.

Fourth-graders Blake Siegwarth and Nic Bruya created this Lewis and Clark matchbook poetry.

Project Materials

※ Pencils/pens
※ 5" by 2" pieces of colored card stock or heavy paper
※ Rulers
※ Tape
※ Glue
※ Scissors
※ Empty square tissue box

Poetry Writing

1 Work as a class to choose a topic that students can use as the overriding theme for their matchbook poems. Be sure to select a topic that is fairly broad so that students can have an easier time selecting their subtopics.

2 Work with individual students or pairs to suggest subtopics for their poems.

3 Have students spend some time thinking about their topic and compiling a list of all they know about it.

4 Invite students to decide what type of poem they would like to write (quatrain, couplet, haiku, etc.). Remind them to take the writing space available on the match-book into consideration as they choose.

5 Once students have written drafts of their poems that they are happy with, have them copy their poems onto 2½" by 2" pieces of paper. If you have access to a computer or a typewriter, have students type their poems and then cut them down to size.

"Koalas," by the students in Corrine Richardson's 3rd-grade class, was written as a part of a Matchbook Poetry collection on marsupials.

> Koalas are Marsupials.
> Their fur is fluffy gray.
> They live in warm Australia.
> And like to sleep all day!

"Lewis and Clark," by 4th-grader Blake Siegwarth, was written as part of a Matchbook Poetry collection on exploring the West.

> Lewis and Clark were courageous and brave.
> Only one of their party was lost to his grave.
> They explored the states to claim the land
> And came back with a map designed by their hands.

Project Steps

1 Help students to fold the card-stock pieces at 2", 2¼", and 4½". Be sure they make a hard crease each time and then reopen it.

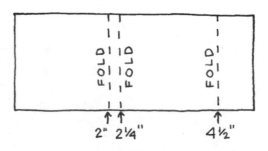

2 Next, students should refold the card stock at the last fold of 4½" and then tape the fold shut along the sides, being careful not to tape over the inside section.

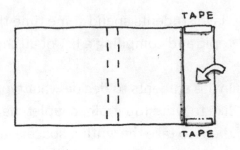

3 Have students glue each poem to the inside of their matchbook as shown, then fold it shut.

Koalas are Marsupials
Their fur is fluffy gray
They live in warm Australia
And like to sleep all day!

4 Invite students to decorate the covers of their matchbooks. Then invite your students to share each other's poems..

5 If you like, store the matchbook poetry projects in a tissue box. Just ask some volunteers to decorate the box in a way that reflects the broad theme the poems cover.

Individual

Paper-Bag Poetry Kite

By Krista Standinger
Tugging, pulling,
Crashing, falling, swirling,
Soaring, flying,
This is fun,
Happiness is here.

Students explore the world from a kite's perspective and record their observations in a form of tanka poem.

Krista Standinger, a 3rd grade student, created this Paper-Bag Poetry Kite about what it might be like to be a kite.

Project Materials

※ Small, lunch-sized paper bags

※ Cardboard

※ Scissors

※ 3 short pieces of string, plus 1 long piece per student

※ Glue

※ Tape

※ Art supplies

Poetry Writing

Tanka (tanhg-kuh) is a classic form of Japanese poetry that dates back at least 1,300 years. Tanka poems are composed of five unrhymed lines. Today's tanka takes on many forms. The tanka poetry presented in this activity counts words instead of syllables. It follows a 2-, 3-,

2-, 3-, 3- words per line format. Like the traditional tanka, the lines of the poem when read together form a single complete thought.

Soaring, flying,
through the air
Flipping, flopping
Not a care
I'm happy now
—*Jenny Challis, Grade 4*

Flying high
Soaring among birds
Wind whipping
Dizzy, giddy sensations
No string attached
—*Joyce Standing's 5th-graders*

1 Ask students to close their eyes and to try to imagine what it would be like to be a kite. Encourage them to think about how it would feel both physically and emotionally.

2 As their imaginations begin to soar, invite students to write down all the words that come to mind on a piece of draft paper.

3 Next, students should combine the words to write a draft of their tanka. Encourage them to play with the words and sounds until they feel their poem is just right.

4 Have students write the final copy of their poems onto a sheet of white paper. Or, if you like, have students compose their final drafts on the computer and then print them out.

> ★ **TEACHER HINT** ★
>
> Invite older students to write traditional Japanese tanka—one straight 31-syllable line of poetry. Or, if you prefer have them write five unrhymed lines following a 5-7-5-7-7 format.

Project Steps

1 Have each student trace and cut a 3" circular piece of cardboard. Then ask students to trace and cut a 2" circular center to form a ring.

2 Next, have each student use the cut-out center piece to trace a circle on the bottom of the paper bag. Then have them cut the circle out, leaving an opening in the bottom of the paper bag. Some students may need assistance with cutting.

3 Guide students in winding one end of each short piece of string around the cardboard ring and securing each one with a knot. Once all the strings are attached, have students tie these together.

4 Ask students to tie the long piece of string to the three shorter pieces and then glue the ring around the edges of the opening on the inside of the paper bag so that the strings come out the bottom of the bag.

5 Invite students to paste their poems to the outside of their paper-bag kites and decorate them.

6 Have a kite-flying party. Students can share their poems and then fly their kites for all to see. Be sure to let students know ahead of time that these are not high-flying kites. Rather, they fly behind you as you walk quickly or run.

TRACE AND CUT OUT INNER CIRCLE

RING INSIDE BOTTOM OF BAG

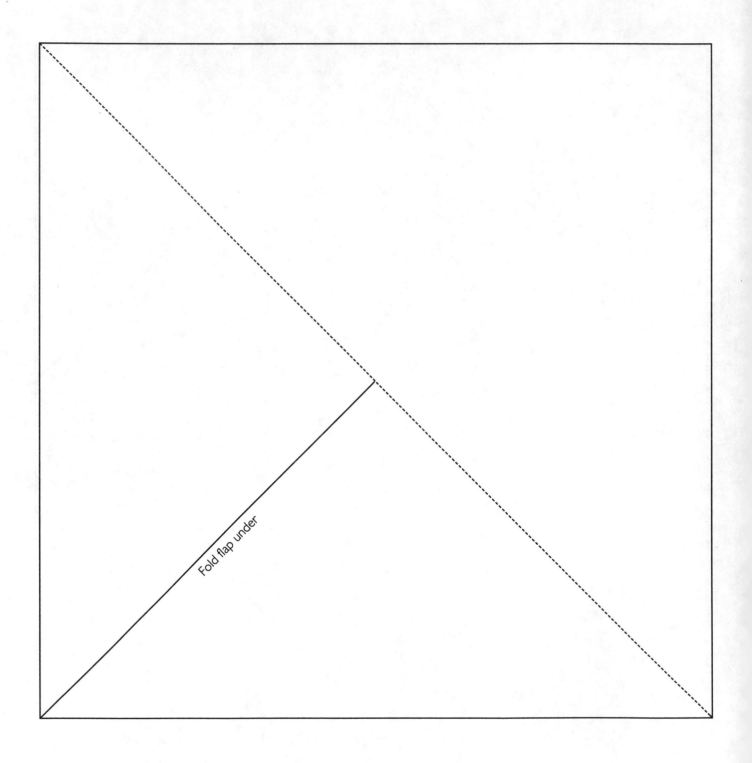

Fold flap under

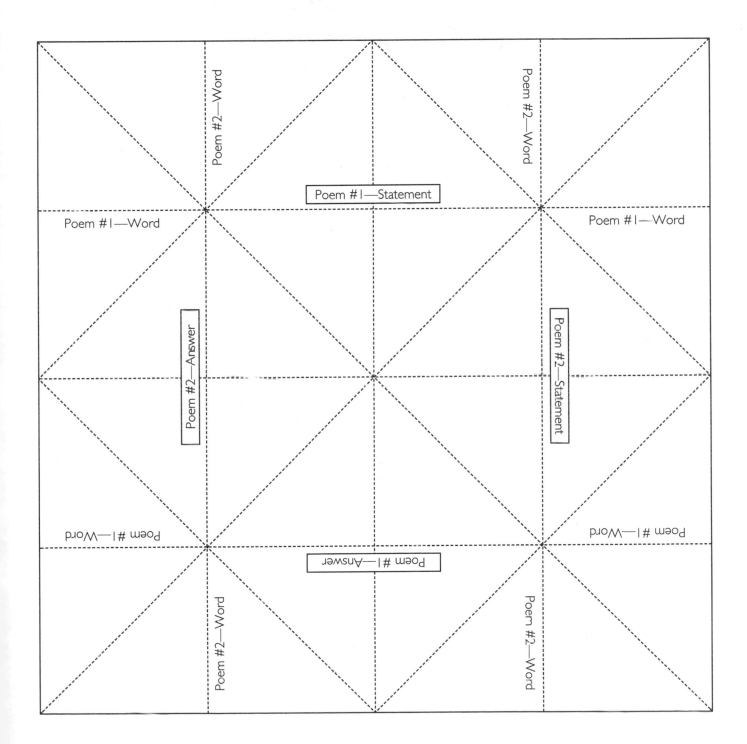

Quick Writing Guidelines for 10 Forms of Poetry

You may find the following guidelines helpful as you explore the poetry writing process with your students.

Acrostic

N—descriptive words
A—descriptive words
M—descriptive words
E—descriptive words

Acrostic Alliteration

T—descriptive words
I—descriptive words
T—descriptive words
L—descriptive words
E—descriptive words

Cinquain

Line 1—one word title

Line 2—two descriptive words

Line 3—three action words

Line 4—four feeling words

Line 5—one word which answers the question. "When I think of the title, I think of . . . ?"

Couplet

Line of poetry that rhymes with line 2
Line of poetry that rhymes with line 1

Freeform

Written in any way students choose to write.

Guess the Person, Place, or Thing

Line 1—descriptive word as clue
Line 2—descriptive word as clue
Line 3—descriptive word as clue
Line 4—descriptive word as clue
Line 5—descriptive sentence as clue
Line 6—answer

Haiku

Line 1—5 syllables
Line 2—7 syllables
Line 3—5 syllables

List

one
descriptive
word
following
another

Number Alliteration

Line 1—line of words that start with the same sound as the *o* in One

Line 2—line of words that start with the same sound as the *t* in Two

Line 3—line of words that start with the same sound as the *th* in Three

Line 4—line of words that start with the same sound as the *f* in Four

Line 5—line of words that start with the same sound as the *f* in Five

Tanka

Line 1—2 words

Line 2—3 words

Line 3—2 words

Line 4—3 words

Line 5—3 words

Quatrain

(abab)

Line 1—line of poetry that rhymes with line 3

Line 2—line of poetry that rhymes with line 4

Line 3—line of poetry that rhymes with line 1

Line 4—line of poetry that rhymes with line 2

(aabb)

Line 1—line of poetry that rhymes with line 2

Line 2—line of poetry that rhymes with line 1

Line 3—line of poetry that rhymes with line 4

Line 4—line of poetry that rhymes with line 3

(abba)

Line 1—line of poetry that rhymes with line 4

Line 2—line of poetry that rhymes with line 3

Line 3—line of poetry that rhymes with line 2

Line 4—line of poetry that rhymes with line 1

Notes